Everything a child needs to know about
BEDWETTING

By
Dr C R Yemula

Health insights 4u
Empowering you through knowledge

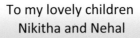

To my lovely children
Nikitha and Nehal

Published in the UK in 2008 by
Health Insights 4U Ltd
60 Bradgate Road, Bedford, MK40 3GB
www.healthinsights4u.com
E mail: info@healthinsights4u.com

ISBN 978-0-9558614-0-6

A catalogue record for this book is available from
the British Library

Please note:
The information presented in the book is intended as a support to
professional advice and care. It is not a substitute
for medical diagnosis or treatment.

Contents

Dear parents and carers,

You may be reassured to know that there are over 500,000 children in the UK who regularly wet the bed. I say this because many parents feel that they are "the only one" to have a child with this common difficulty.

Children too can feel isolated and alone. This is because bedwetting is still not talked about very openly, although we hope that books such as this will improve the situation.

There is information available for parents and carers on bedwetting but very little for children. This book fills such an important gap.

It is written for children to help them to understand about bedwetting, how it affects children and their families and what can be done.

It is important to seek help from your nurse or doctor, as it is a problem that **can** be overcome.

Best wishes,

Penny Dobson
Director of ERIC

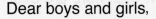

Dear boys and girls,

There are many children all over the world who have bedwetting problems. Bedwetting can happen in all age groups but it is more common in young children.

This book tells the story of Ben and Daisy who both wet the bed and how they eventually get better.

No one is perfect. Some children have asthma and some have diabetes. Don't feel bad about wetting the bed. It is not your fault.

Read the story and share your thoughts with your brothers, sisters, friends and also the grown-ups at home.

Good luck and best wishes,

Dr C R Yemula

Ben is a 6-year-old boy with bedwetting problems and as you read his story, you will get to know more about Ben and how he tries to manage his problems.

Ben is a lovely boy with brown eyes and dark hair. He lives with his parents in a flat near the town centre. He has a little sister called Becky, who is 4 years old and a brother, James, aged 8 years.

Ben's mum is a teacher and his dad works as a manager in a shop. Both Ben and James like to be active and walk to their local school. They have a big park nearby and often go out to play games. Ben likes football and is now learning to play tennis.

Ben's mum is worried that Ben still wets his bed at night. She took him to see their family doctor, Dr Goodman.

He examined Ben and said that he was a healthy boy.
He checked Ben's urine sample, which was normal. He then wrote a letter to Dr Best asking him to see Ben in his clinic.

Dr Goodman

Dr Best runs a special clinic for children with bedwetting problems.

Clinic

Can I help you?

Miss Direct

RECEPTIONIST

Dr Best
Enuresis* Clinic

10

*Enuresis means bedwetting

Two weeks later, Ben and his parents went to see Dr Best in the clinic. It was a big room with lots of toys and puzzles. Ben sat down and started colouring in pictures.

Dr Best wanted to know more about his bedwetting. He asked Ben how many drinks he has every day and if there is anyone else in the family who also wets the bed.

Dr Best

Mum said Ben has his own bedroom. Every night Ben wets his bed before midnight and the bed sheets are soaking wet. Although he tries hard to be dry, he can't help it. He sleeps heavily and can't wake up at night even after wetting his bed.

Ben usually has 3 to 4 drinks during the day and likes to have blackcurrant or hot chocolate in the evenings.

Ben's mum remembered that she herself wet the bed until she was 8 years old.

11

At home, Ben's brother James often teases him that he is still wetting the bed. Ben doesn't like this at all. He feels very sad and embarrassed.

James

His mum wakes him at night around 10 o' clock to take him to the toilet, which is not helpful. Ben still wets the bed every night.

Ben often cries after wetting the bed and tries to hide his wet bed sheets.

His mum knows that it is not his fault but his dad says "Ben, you are too old, stop being lazy". Sometimes his mum and dad argue about this at home.

Mr Cross

Ben,
You are a big boy,
Stop wetting the bed!

12

How is Ben doing at school?

Ben is a popular boy at school. He has lots of friends. He is always polite and well behaved in his class.

He is good at reading, writing and spelling. He is very attentive, listens to stories and comes out with brilliant ideas. His teacher says "It is a pleasure to teach Ben".

Mrs Wise

Ben is missing sleep-overs

Ben's uncle lives in Ireland with his wife and son Jack, aged 7 years. Ben's parents are planning to visit the family during the Easter holidays. They are worried Ben might be embarrassed and possibly teased by his cousin if he wets the bed.

Ben's best friend, Sam, is having a sleep-over for his birthday party next month. Although Ben wants to go, he is scared that his friends will find out about his secret.

13

What did Ben's parents do?

Ben's parents asked Dr Best why Ben was still wetting the bed and how they can help him. They asked Dr Best lots of other questions.

Is it a common problem?

Dr Best said bedwetting is a common problem in children and both boys and girls can wet the bed.

Don't feel bad.
There are lots of children who wet the bed.

You are not alone!

Did you know in a class of 30 children...

- At the age of 5 years: 4 to 5 children wet the bed.
- At the age of 10 years: There are at least 2 children who wet the bed.
- Occasionally, some teenagers still wet the bed.

Miss Sentence

14

Is it a common problem?

Dr Best said that in the clinic he sees lots of children with bedwetting problems.

They come from different ethnic backgrounds – European, Asian and African children.

Does it run in families?

Bedwetting can be passed down from parents to children. If one or both the parents have wet the bed, then their child could also wet the bed.

Grandpa John

Did you know I used to wet the bed as a child?

15

Dr Best said there are three main reasons why children wet the bed. A child may have one or a combination of the following:

1 The child makes a lot of urine at night

2 The child has an overactive bladder

3 The child is not able wake up at night

Z Z Z

Jack Snorre

Stress

Some children who are usually dry at night may start wetting the bed when they are upset or stressed.
For example, this could happen if their parents are separating or if they are being bullied at school.

We all have two kidneys which collect water from the food and drink we take everyday. The waste water then becomes urine and goes to the bladder via tiny tubes.

The bladder is like a balloon and when it is full, it sends out a signal to your brain. Your brain then tells your bladder if it is OK to wee.

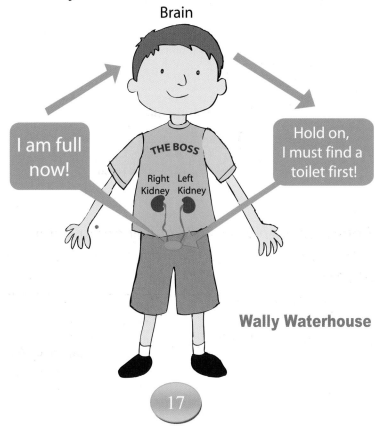

Wally Waterhouse

Did you know? Our brain makes a chemical called Vasopressin and that more is made at night. This is to help your kidneys make less urine overnight.

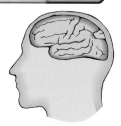

However, some children who wet the bed may have low levels of Vasopressin at night. As a result, they produce lots of urine, which the bladder can't hold and this spills over causing bedwetting.

Soon after going to sleep, these children wet the bed and tend to leave large wet patches.

18

What is an overactive bladder?

Here the bladder is a lot more active and 'twitchy'. The bladder can only hold small amounts of urine and empties before it is full.

Twitchy bladder

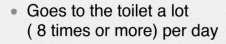

The child with an overactive bladder may have one or more of the following difficulties:

Danny Dash

- Goes to the toilet a lot (8 times or more) per day

- Often rushes to the toilet

- Wets during the day time

- Passes small amounts of urine

- Wets more than once at night

Gary Yourin

Dr Best said that some children like Ben, who wet the bed, have difficulty waking up from sleep. They can't wake up even when their bladder is full.

A few children are scared of the dark at night and they don't want to get up to go to the toilet. It would be helpful to have the landing light on in the corridor. Sometimes a torch light can come in handy!

Mr Bladder

Come on, can't you feel I am full? Wake up now, I need to be emptied!

Sleepy Sam

What did Dr Best do?

Dr Best checked Ben's weight, height and blood pressure. After examining him, Dr Best said that Ben is a healthy weight and that he is a tall boy!

He then talked about some simple things to help Ben stop wetting the bed.

What should Ben do?

- Have at least 6 to 7 drinks each day. This can be water or squash.

- Try cutting out fizzy drinks, tea, coffee, hot chocolate and blackcurrant to see if it helps. Did you know these drinks make our kidneys produce more urine?

Dr Best gave Ben a list of things to do.

- Go to the toilet for a wee just before bedtime. Do it again after brushing your teeth, so that you empty your bladder completely.

- Get up at night to go to the toilet if you feel like passing urine.

I need a wee-wee

- Have the light on in the corridor or carry a torch if you are afraid of the dark.

- Keep a diary of the dry nights so that you can check your progress.

- Eat plenty of fruit and vegetables. This will help you to avoid constipation. (Constipation means trouble passing poo)

Dr Best then talked about bladder training.

Ready, steady, wee…

Mr Loo

- During the day, go to the toilet every couple of hours.

- Don't rush in and out of the toilet. Relax, take your time and empty your bladder.

Charlie Drinkwater

- Ask your mum or dad to help you with a special chart. This is to record your drinking and how much urine you pass during the daytime.

- Measure the amount of urine you pass and see if this matches with your bladder capacity.

Miss Wee Wee

- You can easily work out your bladder capacity, which is the amount of urine your bladder should hold.

Ben aged 6 years

$6 + 1 = 7$

$7 \times 30 = 210$ mls

Bladder

Bladder capacity = (Age + 1) x 30
In millilitres

Dr Best said that Ben can try an alarm to help him stop wetting the bed. Dr Best gave Ben the following information:

There are two kinds of alarms:

- Body alarm

- Bed mat alarm

See page **34** to find out what the alarms look like

The alarm will help you to recognise the signals when your bladder becomes full at night. It makes a noise as soon as you wet.

You then need to wake up, switch off the alarm and go to the toilet to empty your bladder. Your parents need to wake you up if you are still sleeping.

ZZZZZ

Mr Snooze

You can help mum or dad change the wet bed sheets and switch the alarm back on, before you go back to sleep.

More about the alarm

A few weeks after using the alarm, you may have smaller wet patches before becoming dry at night. Sometimes it takes many weeks before you become completely dry at night.

Mrs Record

After you have been dry for 2 weeks, the alarm can be switched off to see if you can still stay dry without it. About 7 out of 10 children become dry after using the alarm.

Are there any problems?

- Children aged between 6 to 7 years may need a lot of support from parents.

- It is important that whole family knows about the alarm so that they get used to the sound of the alarm.

Will Wacup

What about medicines?

Dr Best said that there is a medicine called Desmopressin, which can help Ben to stay dry at night.

The medicine works on your kidneys to make less urine at night. This allows your bladder to hold on to urine and stops you from wetting the bed.

This medicine comes in two forms, as a melt and as a tablet. The melt form, as the name suggests, quickly melts in the mouth. It is taken at bedtime and no water is needed. However, you can have a small sip of water with the tablet.

When to take the medicine?

You can take the medicine:

- Daily at bedtime
- When going for sleep-overs, school trips, camps or holidays
- When the alarm is not helpful

More about the medicine

Ben's parents asked whether the medicine helps all children to stop wetting the bed.

Dr Best said the medicine can help around 7 out of 10 children to have more dry nights.

It is important to stop the medicine for a week, every 3 months to see if the child still needs it.

Breaktime

Are there any problems?

Dr Best said most children don't have any problems. Sometimes a child may develop a bit of a tummy ache or a headache. However, if a child has a bad tummy ache or feels sick, they should stop the medicine and the parents need to contact the doctor for advice.

Remember: Always take the medicine as advised by your doctor or nurse.
At night, you can have small sips of drink if you feel thirsty but don't drink lots of fluids.

27

What did Ben's parents do?

Ben's parents are worried that Ben is not a happy boy. He feels sad as he is still wetting the bed whilst his brother and sister are both dry. They often tease him at home. He is keen to go to Sam's house for the sleep-over next month.

Dr Best asked Ben whether he would like to try the tablet or the melt form of the medicine. Ben said he would prefer the melt and started taking it at bedtime.

What happened next?

3 months later… Ben is now a proud boy with a huge smile on his face.

Ben and his mum went to see Dr Best in the clinic. They brought Ben's diary to show his progress. He was completely dry every night for the past 4 weeks.

Well done

He has had lots of fun and a fantastic sleep-over at Sam's house.

What did Dr Best do?

Dr Best asked Ben's mum to gradually reduce and then stop the medicine. Ben should continue to have 6 to 7 drinks a day and eat plenty of fruit and vegetables.

Ben's mum asked what to do if Ben wets again after stopping the medicine. Dr Best said that, like lots of children, Ben can have continuous dry nights. However, he can take the medicine again if he starts wetting the bed.

How is Ben doing now?

After 2 months… Ben has a dry bed every night. He doesn't take the medicine anymore. He is now a happy and confident boy who wakes up every morning with a bright smile!

Dr Best gave him a certificate for trying his best to stay dry.

Daisy is 8 years old and lives with her parents in a small village. She is a pretty girl with blue eyes and light brown hair.

Like Ben, Daisy also wets the bed. She wets about 4 to 5 nights a week. She sleeps through and does not wake after wetting the bed. Occasionally she gets up at night to go to the toilet.

She is due to start a new school. She wants to be dry and would do anything to get better.

Daisy sees Mrs Smart

Daisy's mum made an appointment to see Mrs Smart, who is a special nurse for children with bedwetting problems.

Mrs Smart

Mum said Daisy doesn't drink enough although she eats healthily. Sometimes Daisy has trouble passing hard poo. She doesn't rush to the toilet or wet herself during the day.

Mum told Mrs Smart that Daisy's uncle also wet the bed until he was 10 years old.

Mr Waterfall

How does Daisy feel?

Daisy feels guilty and is too embarrassed to talk about bed wetting. She has to wear pull-ups at night when going on a family holiday. She avoids sleep-overs and is scared that her friends might find out about her bedwetting.

31

What did Mrs Smart do?

Mrs Smart tested Daisy's urine sample and said it was fine.

Looking at the chart completed by Daisy's mum, Mrs Smart said Daisy only has 3 to 4 drinks per day. Although she doesn't drink enough, she drinks mainly water and not fizzy drinks.

Mrs Smart asked Daisy to do the following things:

- Have at least 6 to 7 drinks every day.

- Eat plenty of high fibre foods – fruit and vegetables.
  This will help you to pass soft poo.

- During the daytime, go to the toilet every 2 hours and don't rush in the toilet.

- At bedtime go to the toilet and empty your bladder completely.

- At night, try and avoid wearing pull-ups

What did Mrs Smart do?

Mrs Smart talked about the medicine and alarm treatments.

Both Daisy and her mum wanted to try the alarm. Mrs Smart then explained about the two kinds of alarms.

1 **Body alarm** - This is also called a **Mini-alarm**.

It has a small noise box and a detector (like a wire) which is tucked into your underpants. As soon as you wet, the alarm makes a loud sound or vibrates (a buzzing feeling) to help you wake up.

2 **Bed mat alarm** - Here you sleep on the alarm mat at night.

When the alarm goes off you need to get up to go to the toilet and empty your bladder. The wet bed sheets need to be changed and the alarm should be switched on before you go back to sleep.

Body alarm

Mr Tick-Tock

Bed mat alarm

Mrs Smart asked Daisy's mum to use this chart to see how well she is doing with the alarm.

Day	Alarm triggered			Dry bed Yes / No	Any Comments?
	Time	Child woke up Yes / No	Size of wet patch Small Medium Large		
Monday					
Tuesday					
Wednesday					
Thursday					
Friday					
Saturday					
Sunday					

Daisy started to have more drinks every day, mainly water and squash. She now goes to the toilet regularly and doesn't have any trouble passing poo.

Mrs Smart gave Daisy a bed mat alarm to take home. At the beginning, Daisy found it hard to wake up to the sound of the alarm. Her mum and dad woke her up whenever the alarm went off. Gradually, she started waking to the alarm by herself and she was having smaller and fewer wet patches.

Daisy kept a diary of her dry nights. After a couple of months, she managed 2 weeks of dry nights and the alarm was switched off. She has continued to stay dry at night.

She went to see Mrs Smart in the clinic and received a certificate for doing so well. Daisy is now a very happy girl as she no longer wets the bed.

Can you colour the pictures?

Billy the Builder

Robbie the Robot

Bobby Playball

Lilly and Milly

Mr B Kwick

Can you find
the answers in
60 seconds?

1

2

Now go to next page to check your answers

Remember...

- Have 6 to 7 drinks every day
- Drink water or squash
- Try cutting out fizzy drinks, tea, coffee, hot chocolate and blackcurrant, to see if it helps

Water is cool

Peter Drinkmore

- Try to go for a wee 6 times a day

Lucy Waterloo

I am the boss of my bladder

I'm ready when you are!

Mr Flush

- Go for a wee as soon as you feel the need
- Relax and take your time
- Empty your bladder completely

James Pond

Think positive

I want to be dry
I can be dry
I will be dry

Jennie Goodnight

Now go to next page...

Have you got all the correct answers? Check it out!		
1. The Sun is red	4. The bird is violet	7. The tree's hole is closed
2. Ladder's 3 rungs missing	5. The bush is pink	8. One boy's hair is black
3. One boy's shirt is green	6. The flower is different	9 & 10. One boy's hair and hat are different

CHECK YOUR PROGRESS

Cosmic Castle

You need to colour the area around each number after having a dry night. Start with '1' and continue until you complete all the numbers up to '30'.

Check your progress

Week	1	2	3	4	5	6
Monday						
Tuesday						
Wednesday						
Thursday						
Friday						
Saturday						
Sunday						

Congratulations for achieving dry nights!

You can start the week by putting a sticker for every dry night. This can be a smiley face, a star or one of your favourite stickers.

Dear boys and girls

Ben has prepared a quiz for you to check how much you understood about bedwetting problems. There are 10 questions and you can score 10 points for each correct answer.

1 Bedwetting occurs in boys only

True   False

2 You should wear nappies or pull ups to stop bedwetting

True   False

3 At the age of 5 years, in a class of 30 there may be
.... boys and girls who wet the bed

4 Name 2 causes of bedwetting

1) ....2).............................

5 You need to have ......drinks (water or squash) every day

6 Name 3 drinks you try cutting out, to see if it helps

1)....................2)......................3...........................

7 Name two methods to treat bedwetting - fill in the blanks

1) - - - - m   2) M - d - - - - e

Quiz Master

8 Name 2 types of alarms

1)..2)..

9 How does an alarm help children with bedwetting?
....

10 How does desmopressin (medicine) help children with bedwetting?
....

Mr Scorewell

Check your score

0 - 20 points ....Sorry, You need to read the book again ★

30 - 40 points ....Not bad, you need to read a bit more ★★

50 - 60 points............ Good, you are getting there slowly ★★★

70 - 80 points............. Well done, keep up the good work ★★★★

90 - 100 points..........Excellent, you are a fantastic reader! ★★★★★

Check your answers

1. False 2. False 3. 4 to 5 children
4. Low levels of vasopressin and overactive bladder
5. Six 6. Tea, coffee, blackcurrant 7. Alarm, medicine
8. Body alarm and bed mat alarm 9. See page 24
10. See page 26

WORD Search

Q	E	B	O	O	K	S	T	D	G
S	N	L	I	V	L	T	O	I	N
K	I	M	Y	E	N	I	R	U	I
X	A	L	E	R	T	U	C	Q	T
D	R	P	N	A	X	R	H	A	T
R	B	T	D	C	S	F	M	L	E
I	V	R	I	T	Z	U	R	Y	W
N	Y	A	K	I	Y	R	A	I	D
K	I	M	Y	V	F	D	L	S	E
S	M	S	R	E	D	D	A	L	B

Word Search by Candis Zenna

- Bedwetting
- Brain
- Alarm
- Mat
- Kidney
- Dry
- Bladder
- Urine
- Books
- Drinks
- Relax
- Smart
- Overactive
- Diary
- Fruits
- Sleep
- Torch
- Alert

Books of interest

Books for parents / carers

- Bedwetting: A Guide for Parents by Penny Dobson, published by ERIC 1988, republished 2006.

- Your Child's Alarm by Jennifer Adams, published by ERIC 1998, republished 2004.

Books for children

- You and Your Alarm by Jennifer Adams, published by ERIC 1990, republished 2006.

- Talk about bedwetting by June Rogers, published by PromoCon 2004.

For more information

www.eric.org.uk

ERIC stands for 'Education and Resources for Improving Childhood Continence'. It is a national charity providing support and up-to-date information to parents/carers, children and young people about continence problems.

Helpline no 0845 370 8008

Mr P C Webb

Other useful websites

www.promocon.co.uk

www.stopbedwetting.co.uk

46